Easy words to read
Goose on the loose

Phil Roxbee Cox
Illustrated by Stephen Cartwright
Edited by Jenny Tyler

Language consultant:
Marlynne Grant
BSc, CertEd, MEdPsych, PhD, AFBPs, CPsychol

There is a yellow duck to find on every page.

First published in 2001 by Usborne Publishing Ltd. Usborne House, 83–85 Saffron Hill, London EC1N 8RT, England. www.usborne.com
Copyright © 2001 Usborne Publishing Ltd.

Goose is on a scooter.
She can't stay and play.

She's a goose on the loose.
"Get out of my way!"

HONK!

She almost knocks down Rooster Ron.

"Get out of my way!"
Goose goes scooting on.

HONK!
HONK!

5

Goose is scooting to Ted's shed...

THE

ZOO

She almost scoots
right into Toad.

"Look out, behind you. Watch out, Ted!"

Ted ends up in his flower bed.

Goose goes scooting down the road.

Toad groans and drops a heavy load.

GROAN!

The cows all moo.

the pigeons coo.

The brown owl says,
"too-wit-too-woo".

Now Goose is heading for...

Look out! Goose is on the loose.

She upsets a bunch of kangaroos...

...and startles a flock of cockatoos.

There are shouts of "hiss!"
and shouts of "boo!"

Then snarls and whoops
and a hullabaloo.

Goose must be stopped! What shall we do?"

But Goose has stopped, and feels a fool.

She's landed in the penguin pool!